ONE

ONE

A Small Group Journey Toward
Life-Changing Community

Leader Guide

Nick Cunningham
with Trevor Miller

Abingdon Press / Nashville

ONE Leader Guide
A Small Group Journey Toward Life-Changing Community
By Nick Cunningham with Trevor Miller
Copyright © 2016 by Abingdon Press
All rights reserved.

Scripture quotations in this publication, unless otherwise indicated, are from the Common English Bible, © Copyright 2011 by Common English Bible, and are used by permission.

Scripture quotations noted NRSV are taken from the New Revised Standard Version of the Bible, copyright 1989, Division of Christian Education of the National Council of the Churches of Christ in the United States of America. Used by permission. All rights reserved.

ISBN-13: 9781501816468

16 17 18 19 20 21 22 23 24 25—10 9 8 7 6 5 4 3 2 1

Manufactured in the United States of America

Contents

Introduction

A WORD TO YOU, LEADER

That word *leader* can be quite intimidating, can't it? It suggests that you are supposed to be out in front, that you have to be more together than everyone else. I'm happy to tell you, however, that you don't have to be intimidated. To be sure, the Bible makes it clear that leadership is a high calling, not to be undertaken lightly. But the Scriptures do not suggest that you have to pretend to be something you're not. You aren't perfect, and that is just fine. You don't have it all together, and you don't have to. You are a work in progress.

That word *progress* is an important one, because it points us to the two most important things that are at the heart of Christian leadership, especially in regards to leading a small group community. The first is that a person in progress is someone who hasn't arrived. He or she isn't finished yet. There are always places in our lives that need work and perhaps a deeper exposure to the transforming love of God. Leaders are aware of these places, and they don't try to hide them from the people they are leading. At the same time, being aware of their own areas where growth is needed, they are committed to offering grace to others.

The second aspect of being a work in progress is that you must indeed be *in progress*. Acknowledging our own areas of weakness does not mean we accept them, but that we put the grace of God to work in our lives. We must be striving to get better, to be transformed more and more into Christ's likeness. This is what the people we lead need to see from us. They need to see in us an open honesty about the ways in which we don't have it all together. But they also need to see a hopeful pursuit to embrace the fullness of what God has made available to us in Jesus Christ.

Practically speaking, there are three practices that you as a leader can adopt in order to lead well.

The first is to pray for your people by name on a daily basis. I'm sure there are all sorts of ways in which they need God to work in their lives. At the same time, the overall connection of your group depends not only on the time you spend together but also on the way in which God works in all of you throughout the week. Ask God to remind and reinforce what you are learning together throughout the week and to create in all of you a spirit of anticipation for your time with one another.

The second practice is that of asking questions. Someone once told me that solutions should be discovered and not imposed. When people can discover the truth of something themselves, they tend to stay much more committed to it. Instead of trying to solve issues that come up, how can you as a leader help guide your group to solutions instead? Asking good questions can be a great way to accomplish this. At the same time, don't feel like you have to stick only to the questions provided in the student journal or in this leader guide. They serve as a guide and place to start, but you may find yourself wanting to ask a different set of questions. If that is the case, do it! Maybe even spend some time in preparation each week coming up with a few supplemental questions for each discussion time based on what you know about the people in your group and the various things they are dealing with.

Third, as leaders we have to be willing to "bleed first." We will talk some more about this later on in the study, but someone in the group has to be willing to get honest and real first in order to set the tone. Guess what? More than likely it will have to be you. Don't worry, though. Vulnerability tends to be contagious, and once you show some courage the rest of your group will follow suit. Just be aware and recognize those moments when you may have to bleed first in order to get the ball rolling.

Each session of this leader guide contains clear instructions to help you lead your group through the ONE Curriculum. It is important for you to read through each week's session in the leader guide and in the journal in advance so that you are well prepared. Note also what materials you'll need to have available, and be sure to bring those to your group meeting or ask another group member to bring them.

As it says in the journal, your group's time together will be divided into two four-week sessions. During the first four weeks, you will use the videos and teaching content in the journal to explore the scriptural foundations of Christ-centered community, as well as the Core Practices and Core Postures that will help shape your group into such a community. The first four sessions all begin with some key teachings about these aspects of Christ-centered community. Be sure that you and your fellow group members read over this material in advance, so that you are well prepared for your group meeting.

During the second four weeks, you will put into practice what you have learned, developing a covenant statement based on the three Core Practices and creating some ground rules that reflect the three Core Postures. There is no teaching content to read for these chapters, and there are no videos to introduce the sessions. Instead, your own conversations with one another will be the main focus, preparing you to continue meeting on your own after the eighth week.

At the end of the final chapter, you will find some suggestions for continuing your time together, which involve finishing your covenant statements and ground rules and sharing your stories with one another. I encourage you to look at these right now, so that you and your group can be thinking early on about how you will continue living in Christ-centered community.

Part 1:

WEEKS 1–4

Session 1:

ONE LIFE

PREPARATION

As you prepare for this first session, read through the description of each activity and discussion and familiarize yourself with it. You might wish to mark pages in the journal and the relevant passages that you will discuss, so that you can locate them easily. View the video for this session in advance, making note of important points that you want to discuss with the group.

There are a few materials that you need to gather beforehand. First, each member of your group will need a copy of ONE Journal. If everyone does not already have their copy, bring enough copies for each person. They will take these home and bring them back during each week of the ONE Curriculum. It may also be a good idea to have a couple of extra copies on hand in case someone forgets his or her journal.

Second, bring a supply of pens or pencils, enough for each person in your group to have one. They will use these to write or draw in their journals during the session.

Finally, you may wish to have a few Bibles on hand in case you want to refer to specific passages. Usually, the passages that you work with directly will be printed in the ONE Journal, but you may find that you wish to look up others as well.

Arrive to the meeting area early to set up the video for viewing. Greet your fellow group members as they arrive, and start on time.

STARTING OUT
(5 minutes)

God has created humans to exist in relationship with one another. That idea is central to this study, which is designed to guide and reinforce the formation of relationships among members of your small group. That has to start on day one with all of you getting to know one another. Each participant in your group comes from a different background and has a different story. In order to break the ice and begin to build strong connections among yourselves, take time to ask one another the questions under the "Starting Out" section of the journal on page 20. The questions are printed here also for your reference:

1. What is your name? Where are you from? What would you like to share about your family or home life?

2. What do you hope to accomplish by being a part of this ONE study?

Ask all participants to turn to page 20, and read the two questions out loud. Ask for a volunteer to respond, and move clockwise until the entire group has had a chance to answer.

Allow plenty of time for this; don't rush it. This is not a beginning activity that must be done before the "real work" can begin. The real work begins right here! Remind the group to listen actively to one another. As the group leader, it's important that you model this behavior. Make a note of each person's responses, and ask one or two follow-up questions where appropriate.

THE THREE QUESTIONS
(10 minutes)

After you complete the "Starting Out" section, turn to the Three Questions. You'll ask and answer the Three Questions at the beginning of each week's meeting. Here they are:

1. What are you grateful for?

2. What are you anxious about?

3. What are you learning?

Each person in your group will answer one or more of these questions every week. A key goal of this curriculum is to get you all talking—really talking—about your spiritual lives. These three questions give you some common vocabulary for doing that, sharing more than surface-level details and asking about what's going on in your inner life. For more information on the Three Questions, turn to page 33 in the journal and read the section entitled "A Word About Those Three Questions."

Ask your group members to turn to page 21 in the student journal. Ask a volunteer to read the Three Questions out loud. Explain to the group that you all will begin each class meeting with the Three Questions. Remind them how important this will be to help you begin to develop deep relationships.

Invite all group participants to answer <u>one</u> of the Three Questions, using one of the methods below to help you determine which question to answer.

Method 1: Choose one person in the group to begin, and ask him or her one of the Three Questions (you as the leader choose which question). After he or she has responded, that person will choose the next person, asking him or her another of the Three Questions (the first person will choose which question). Then that person will choose the next person and the next question. Continue in this manner until everyone has responded, with you as the leader answering last.

Method 2: Print the Three Questions on small slips of paper and put them into a hat or bowl. Beginning with a volunteer, ask each person to select one piece of paper from the hat or bowl and answer the question on it. Then proceed counter-clockwise until the whole group has responded.

Method 3: Begin with a volunteer, who will choose which of the three questions to answer. Proceed counter-clockwise until the whole group has responded to one of the question, with each person deciding for himself or herself which question to answer.

As the group leader, it's up to you to set the tone for this practice each week. It might not happen right away, but it's important that you all take these questions seriously as an occasion to open your spiritual lives toward one another. As you continue over the next several weeks, ideally you will see individuals grow more comfortable with these questions and give deeper, more thoughtful answers.

WATCH THE VIDEO
(18 minutes)

To serve as a transition into the rest of this week's discussion, play the video titled "One Life." Ask the following questions for group discussion:

Ask: In your experience, are your favorite moments connected to your favorite people? Give an example or two that come to your mind.

Ask: In the video, Nick mentioned that God is Trinity. What does this say about relationships and the image of God?

Ask: How does this change your understanding of the role of relationships with other people in your own faith life?

STUDY THE SCRIPTURES
(15 minutes)

Ask group members to turn to page 22 in the journal. Explain that you will spend a few minutes reading over the two passages, Acts 2:42-47 and Acts 4:32-37. Invite group members to make notes on these passages in the space provided, using the following questions as prompts (these are also printed in the journal):

1. What parts of the community described in these verses do you find attractive? Why?

2. What characteristics of these early believers do you find the same in each passage?

3. What does it means to live in community with "one heart and mind"?

4. What makes this type of community so elusive in our culture today?

Allow seven or eight minutes for members to read and respond individually in the journal. Then discuss these four questions as a group.

In answering the questions and leading the discussion, be sure to refer back to the relevant section on pages 11–14 in the journal. Remember, Luke is not only describing how this community lived but also saying something quite profound about who they were. By quoting Jeremiah 32 and Deuteronomy 15, Luke is declaring that this early group of Jesus followers was in fact the true covenant people of God. What identified them as such was their commitment to a shared life with one another.

A great place to steer the conversation is the question of whether or not we as the church today still use these same identifiers. Conclude this discussion with the following question:

In a highly individualistic society, what would we tend to say identifies us as the "people of God?" Would you say most church goers are committed to a community like we see in Acts 2 and 4? Why or why not?

THE ALLURE OF INDIVIDUALISM
(10 minutes)

Ask group members to turn to pages 25–28 in the journal, reminding them of the discussion on individualism on pages 15–16. Pay specific attention to the part about how individualism has influenced what we believe about salvation.

Ask group members to write or draw in the space provided the ways that individualism is evident in each of these areas of our lives: Family, Friendship, Workplace, and Faith Community. Using a watch to keep time, allow <u>one minute</u> for each area, for four minutes total. Even if members have more to write or draw, instruct them to move to the next area when the minute is up.

After this speed-brainstorming exercise, take time to discuss the following questions:

Ask: What did you discover about individualism in your own life through this exercise?

Ask: How does this compare with the picture of the early church in Acts 2:42-47 and 4:32-37 that we just read and discussed?

Ask: What might our individualism be causing us to miss out on?

EXPERIENCING GOD TOGETHER
(15 minutes)

Ask group members to turn to pages 29–31 in the student journal. Ask them to read the three biblical passages that have been printed and consider the following question (this is also printed in the journal):

Ask: In each passage, what are some aspects of our life with God that we experience more fully together rather than on our own?

Allow seven or eight minutes for everyone to read, think, and make notes in the space provided in the journal. Then discuss the question.

Be sure to refer back to the examples given on pages 16-19 of the journal to help spark conversation around similar experiences each of you have had.

Conclude your discussion with the following question:

Ask: Based on your reading and our discussion, is a commitment to a shared life with other followers of Jesus something that is optional or is it essential? Why? Why is it important for us to wrap our brains around this notion of individualism at the very beginning of our time together?

ONE CHALLENGE
(5 minutes)

Relationships are organic, and therefore they must be birthed and sustained with intention. This week's challenge is for everyone in the group to spend some one-on-one time together with one other person in your group. Refer to the description of the challenge on page 32 of the student journal.

Instruct each group member to pair up with another group member, ensuring that everyone (including yourself) is a part of a pair. If there are an odd number of people, form one group of three. Group members should pair up with someone that they do not know very well. Two best friends, in other words, should not be in a pair together.

One way to form pairs is to assign each person a number and then write the numbers on little pieces of paper. Put the pieces of paper into a hat or bowl, then mix them up and draw two numbers out. Those people will be paired up. If two people are paired up who know each other well, simply put their numbers back and draw again. Repeat this process until everyone has been assigned a pair.

Allow a few minutes for the pairs to set a day and time for their one-on-one meeting and exchange contact information if they do not already have it.

CLOSE THE MEETING
(2 minutes)

Before everyone leaves, be sure to nail down the logistics of when and where you will meet next. Also, point everyone's attention to the week-long devotional starting on the page 33 of the student journal. There will be one of these each week that will either reinforce something you learned previously or prepare you for the following week's conversation.

Ask a volunteer to close with a prayer.

Session 2:

ONE MIND

PREPARATION

Read through the description of each activity and discussion, and familiarize yourself with the session plan. If you will find it helpful, mark pages in the journal and the relevant passages that you will discuss. View the video for this session in advance, making note of important points that you want to discuss with the group.

Gather pens or pencils, extra copies of the journal, and Bibles to have on hand to assist you in the discussion.

Arrive to the meeting area early to set up the video for viewing, and be sure that you start the session right on time.

THE THREE QUESTIONS

(10 minutes)

This past week's daily devotional prepared you and the group to answer the first of the Three Questions. Remind everyone of the importance of the Three Questions, the importance of allowing plenty of time, and the importance of actively listening to and engaging one another's responses. Then begin your session by asking each participant the first question:

What are you grateful for?

Go around the room clockwise beginning with a volunteer, or proceed from one person to the next in alphabetical order based on first names. Alternatively, you as the leader can choose the first person to answer, then that person will choose the next person to answer. Proceed in that manner until everyone has answered. You as the leader will respond last.

It's important that you as the group leader model active listening as a part of this process. Ask questions for clarification or other follow-up questions. Comment on interesting points or what speaks to you.

Be sure, however, that the group moves from one person to the next in a timely manner. Try to ensure that you all spend the same amount of time on each person in the group.

ONE CHALLENGE FOLLOW-UP

(5 minutes)

After answering the first of the Three Questions, spend a few moments talking about the group's time connecting one-on-one during the past week. Check in briefly with each pair, asking where they met, for how long, and what they learned about the other person through this exercise. Decide as a group if this is something you want to continue doing throughout the study, or if you want to arrange a different schedule (such as every other week or once a month) based on time constraints. Meeting one-on-one with every group member can be a great way to move past a classroom feel to actually doing life with one another.

WATCH THE VIDEO

(18 Minutes)

Transition to the rest of this week's discussion by watching the video titled "One Mind." Then discuss the following questions as a group:

Ask: How have you observed the difference between a "crowd" and a "community"? What purpose or passion stands at the center of the communities that you have been a part of?

STUDY THE SCRIPTURES

(20 minutes)

Ask group members to turn to page 55 in the ONE Journal. Explain that you will spend a few minutes reading over the two passages, Acts 2:42-47 and Acts 4:32-37. Invite group members to make notes on these passages in the space provided, using the following questions as prompts (these are also printed in the journal):

1. How would you describe the kind of connection among the believers that we see in these two passages?

2. Share a time when you have experienced this kind of connection with other people.

3. What words, phrases, or verses do you think best summarize the purpose around which the early church was gathered?

Allow seven or eight minutes for members to read and responding individually in the journal. Then discuss these three questions as a group.

In answering the questions and leading the discussion, be sure to refer to what was said on pages 43–48 of the journal.

Read this quote from page 46 of the journal out loud to the group:

"In Acts 4, Luke tells us that the apostles continued to testify to the Resurrection not just with words, but with great power. They didn't just tell people about what they had experienced. Their lives, both individually and communally, bore 'powerful witness' to Jesus' resurrection. The community of believers was the very place where the Kingdom of God was advancing, where heaven was crashing to earth."

Ask: If you asked most people what it means to go to church or be the church, how would their answer differ from this quote?

Ask: What does this have to say about the role and importance of our shared life in Christ?

Ask: Why would our relationships with one another be the very place where the kingdom of God is breaking in?

FORWARD, UP, AND OUT

(20 minutes)

Ask a group member to summarize what the author means by each of the three Core Practices, referring to pages 48–52 in the journal if necessary for clarification.

Explain that you will spend some time reflecting individually on what these three Core Practices mean for you and your group. Ask group members to turn to the sections, "Pushing One Another Forward," "Lifting One Another Up," and "Sending One Another Out" on pages 58–65 in the student journal. Call attention to the questions and space for responses in those pages.

Allow three minutes for members (including yourself) to write or draw responses to the first set of questions, under "Pushing One Another Forward." Use a watch or clock to keep the time.

After the three minutes are up, tell the group to switch and begin answering the second set of questions, under "Lifting One Another Up." It is OK if they have not finished answering the first set of questions.

Allow three more minutes, then switch to the final set of questions, under "Sending One Another Out." Again, it is OK if they have not finished answering the second set of questions. Allow three minutes to complete the final set of questions, then call time.

Ask members to share with the group their most interesting, insightful, or surprising response to a question in each of the three sets.

Ask: What did you learn from this exercise?

Remind the group about the development of a covenant statement, which the author describes on pages 52–53 in the journal and which you will work towards in the second half of this curriculum.

Ask: How would the hard work of developing a covenant statement help set the group up to stay committed to these three Core Practices?

Ask: What insights do you have right now about the shape our covenant statement needs to take?

Ask: Out of the three, which Core Practice would come easiest to you? Why? Which one would be the most uncomfortable? Why?

Encourage group members to write down any insights from the discussion about these three Core Practices in the space provided in the journal. Also encourage them to spend some deeper time with these three sets of questions over the coming week, to go a little deeper or answer any they did not respond to during this exercise.

ONE CHALLENGE

(5 minutes)

For this week's ONE Challenge, the focus is action: What are you going to do? Perhaps someone has shared an area in their life where they need accountability, or perhaps where they need some encouragement. Another thought would be to begin to organize an opportunity for you all to serve together.

Ask the group to turn to the ONE Challenge on page 66 of the journal. Ask a volunteer to read the ONE Challenge out loud. Spend a few moments in silent prayer, inviting each person to ask the Holy Spirit to reveal what is the right thing for him or her to do in response to this ONE Challenge.

People may know right now what they plan to do in response to this challenge. Or they may need a couple of more days of discernment before they identify it. Either way is OK. Offer encouragement, and invite members to share with one other group member what they plan to do when they determine it. Tell the group that you will discuss this challenge at the beginning of next week's meeting.

CLOSE THE MEETING

(2 minutes)

Remind the group about the next meeting time and place, as well as the daily devotional for the upcoming week.

Ask a volunteer to close the meeting with a prayer.

Session 3:

ONE HEART

PREPARATION

R ead through the description of each activity and discussion and familiarize yourself with it, marking pages and passages that you will discuss. View the video for this session in advance, making note of the important points that stand out to you.

Bring enough pens for everyone to use to write and draw in their journals, as well as a few Bibles and any extra copies of the journal that you need to have on hand.

For this week, you will also need a large piece of paper with a pen, a markerboard with markers, or an electronic display (such as a computer and projector) so that you can take notes for one of your discussions below.

Arrive to the meeting area early to set up the video and greet your fellow group members as they arrive. Be sure to start on time.

THE THREE QUESTIONS

(10 minutes)

Last week's daily devotionals led you and the group to think about the second of the Three Questions. Just like last week, begin by reminding everyone of the importance of the Three Questions. Encourage the group to go past surface-level responses and be real with one another. Then ask each participant the second question:

What are you anxious about?

Use the same procedure you have used before, either moving clockwise (or counter-clockwise) beginning with a volunteer, or allowing the person who just answered to choose the next person who will respond. Or feel free to devise a different method and experiment a little bit. The important thing is that everyone has a chance to answer the question and that the group spends an equal amount of time on each person, not allowing one person's response to dominate the conversation too much.

As before, you as the leader should pay close attention, providing comments or questions for follow-up to responses. Don't feel like you have to do this with every person, however, especially if others are following your lead and adding questions and comments of their own. By this third week, everyone should be more familiar with this exercise, and it may lead to more natural, organic participation among the group.

ONE CHALLENGE FOLLOW-UP

(5 minutes)

After answering the second of the Three Questions, follow up with the group on last week's ONE Challenge about the one thing each member was going to commit to doing over the past week.

Ask: What did you do in response to this challenge? How did it go? Where did you see God show up as a result of this?

You do not need to spend a lot of time on this exercise—keep it to no more than a few comments per person. But touching base with the group will help everyone process their experience with the ONE Challenge and set the stage for today's conversation.

WATCH THE DVD

(18 minutes)

Transition to the rest of this week's discussion by watching the video titled "One Heart." Then discuss the following question as a group:

Ask: What is the greatest gift that you have ever received? How was the gift evidence of a deep, meaningful connection with someone else?

Ask: Which of the three Core Postures—vulnerability, compassion, or grace—are you best at? Why?

STUDY THE SCRIPTURES

(20 minutes)

Ask group members to turn to page 85 in the journal. Explain that you will spend a few minutes reading over the three passages, Acts 2:42-47; Acts 4:32-37; and Romans 12:9-21. Invite group members to make notes on these passages in the space provided, using the following questions as prompts (these are also printed in the journal):

1. What are some of your most prized possessions? If your house were burning down, what would you save and why?

2. Acts 4:32 says the community of believers "was one in heart and mind." What does oneness of heart mean to you?

3. What word, phrase, or verse in these passages best demonstrates the group's oneness of heart?

4. Romans 12:9-21 has a lot to say about what our love for one another ought to look like. What specific wisdom does it offer in terms of what is required of us in order to be of one heart?

Allow eight to ten minutes for members to read and respond individually in the space provided in the journal. Then invite group members to share their responses and insights on these four questions.

Read this quote from page 79 in the journal out loud to the group:

"Jesus calls us away from our obsession with independence and invites us into communities of interdependence, in which we can let down the masks and allow ourselves to be truly seen."

Ask: How does this encourage you? How does this challenge you?

VULNERABILITY, COMPASSION, AND GRACE

(20 minutes)

In leading a conversation around the following questions, be sure to refer to the teaching on the three Core Postures on pages 78–82 in the journal. Be aware, this discussion may generate some discomfort. We are not used to being vulnerable with other people, and if we are honest, compassion and grace don't exactly come easily to us either.

Something else that may help prepare you for this conversation is a Ted Talk by author and psychologist Brené Brown called "The Power of Vulnerability." You can find a video of the talk at the following website: *www.ted.com/talks/brene_brown_on_vulnerability?language=en*

Try to watch this video before your group meeting, and make notes on any insights it gives you about vulnerability and the other Core Postures. You may also wish to share this with your group. If so, send them the link so that they can view later this week, before your next meeting. Plan to allow a few minutes to discuss this video at the beginning of your next session.

Ask the group to name the three Core Postures from this week's reading, summarizing the meaning of each one of these postures.

Ask: Which of the three Core Postures did you find the most challenging? Why?

Ask: Which of Nick's personal examples resonated with you the most: the awards banquet story, the leaky sink story, or the angry neighbor story? What about this story connected with you?

Instruct group members to turn to pages 90–91 in the journal, where they will find questions to help them reflect individually on these three Core Postures. Allow two minutes each (six minutes total) for group members to respond to the questions in the space provided. Using a watch or clock to keep the time, tell group members when to move to the next question, even if they are not yet finished with the one they're working on. Here are the question (they are also printed in the journal):

1. When have you experienced vulnerability, either opening up to someone or having someone else open up to you? (2 minutes)

2. What can the group do to encourage vulnerability, to make the group a safe space for people to open up and truly share themselves with one another? (2 minutes)

3. How can the group create a culture of compassion and grace toward one another? What practices can you implement to help these postures take root among you as individuals and within the group as a whole? (2 minutes)

After the six minutes are up, invite group members to share their responses.

Remind the group about the teaching on pages 83–84 in the journal about developing ground rules and sharing your stories with one another.

Ask: How can these two things—ground rules and sharing our stories—help us as a group implement and maintain these three Core Postures?

If you have time remaining, begin brainstorming some potential ground rules for you and your group. Be sure that you or a volunteer writes down these insights and ideas, which you can use over the next several weeks as you establish your ground rules during the rest of the curriculum.

ONE CHALLENGE

(5 minutes)

This week's ONE Challenge involves another one-on-one meeting with a fellow group member. The difference this week is that members are encouraged to practice vulnerability, compassion, and grace—to step out of their comfort zone a bit and to share something with the other person that they might not normally share.

In preparing for this challenge, understand that sharing this sort of personal information is very difficult for some people. Let the group know that they don't have to share their deepest and darkest secrets. The community you are aiming for requires trust, and trust doesn't happen overnight. However, setting the precedent by sharing some sense of who you really are will help to ensure that you do connect on a deeper level.

Ask group members to turn to page 92 of the journal and find the ONE Challenge. Ask a volunteer to read the challenge out loud. Encourage the group to make time for these one-on-one meetings during the week, as they are a great step toward learning to practice vulnerability, compassion, and grace.

Instruct group members to form pairs as you did in Session 1, again forming one group of three if there are an odd number of members. Each person should have a different partner than he or she had in the first week. As before, you can ask group member to form pairs on their own, or you can write names (or assigned numbers) on slips of paper and draw them randomly to form the pairs.

Allow a few minutes for each pair to meet each other, arrange a meeting time and place, and exchange contact information.

CLOSE THE MEETING

(2 minutes)

Remind the group about your next session, as well as the daily devotionals for the upcoming week. Ask a volunteer to close the meeting with a prayer.

Session 4:

ONE WAY

PREPARATION

Read through the description of each activity and discussion, and familiarize yourself with the overall session plan. Mark places in the journal that you want to reference in the discussion, and watch the video in advance to note important points.

Gather the supplies that you will need, including pens or pencils for every group member, extra journals if you need them, and Bibles to have on hand. You may find it helpful to use a large piece of paper, markerboard, or projection screen to display notes on your discussions. If this is the case, be sure to have these materials available in your meeting space as well.

Arrive to the meeting area early to set up the video for viewing. Greet your fellow group members as they arrive, and start on time.

THE THREE QUESTIONS

(10 minutes)

The daily devotionals for last week prepared you and the group to answer the third of the Three Questions. By now you should all be getting familiar with this practice, but a quick reminder of its importance still isn't a bad idea. Begin your session by asking each participant the third question:

What are you learning?

Use the same procedure you have used over the past few weeks, either moving clockwise (or counter-clockwise) beginning with a volunteer or allowing the person who just answered to choose the next person who will respond. Or experiment with a new way of proceeding. The important thing is that everyone has a chance to answer the question and that the group spends an equal amount of time on each person, not allowing one person's response to dominate the conversation too much.

This week's question, what are you learning?, is often the most difficult of the three questions for people to answer. Ideally, the devotionals will have helped people think through this a little bit and be ready with an answer. But if people feel stuck, ask them to share something they have learned over the last several weeks together as a result of this study.

ONE CHALLENGE FOLLOW-UP

(5 minutes)

After answering the first of the Three Questions, spend a few moments talking about the group's time connecting one-on-one during the past week. Check in briefly with each pair, asking where they met, for how long, and what they learned about the other person through this exercise.

Ask each pair: How was the experience of practicing vulnerability, compassion, and grace toward one another in a one-on-one setting? How did this affect your ability to get to know the other person?

Again, consider as a group if this is something you want to continue doing throughout the rest of the study, or if you want to arrange a different schedule (such as every other week or once a month) based on time constraints.

WATCH THE VIDEO

(13 minutes)

Transition into this week's discussion by watching the video titled "One Way." Then discuss with the group using the following questions:

Ask: What experience have you had that you have been excited to share with others? What led you to want to share it, and how was it received?

Ask: What prevents us from wanting to share our experience of God in the same way?

STUDY THE SCRIPTURES

(20 minutes)

Ask the group members to turn to pages 110–118 in the journal. Explain that you will be studying some different passages in the Book of Acts that demonstrate in various ways the inside-out nature of God's kingdom.

Instruct group members to recall the teaching about these passages on pages 101–107 of the journal.

Ask: What insights did you find especially interesting about these passages? What did you learn that you didn't know before?

In what follows, you and the group will read through these passages to study them in more depth. Invite group members to take notes on each passage, keeping in mind the following question (which is also printed in the journal):

How do you see the inside-out nature of the kingdom of God demonstrated in these passages?

Ask for a volunteer to read Acts 1:1-9 out loud. Instruct the rest of the group to follow along on page 111 of the journal, making notes about wherever they see the inside-out nature of the kingdom of God.

Ask: Where and how are the people gathered? How do you see God's kingdom pushing the boundaries that the people currently recognize?

Ask for another volunteer to read Acts 8:1-8; 26-35, with the rest of the group following along and making notes on pages 112–113 of the journal.

Ask: What is the result of the church's scattering? Was this a good thing or a bad thing? How did it affect the proclamation of the good news?

Ask for a third volunteer to read Acts 9:1-19, with the rest of the group reading along and making notes on pages 114–115 of the journal.

Ask: What is the significance of Saul's conversion to following Jesus? How do you see the inside-out nature of God's kingdom at work in him?

Next, ask another volunteer to read Acts 10:1-35. Other group members should follow along on pages 116–117 of the journal.

Ask: How does this passage reflect the expansion of God's kingdom? Was it foreshadowed at all in the other three passages we read? Where does God's kingdom go from here?

Finish by discussing the following quotation from page 105 of the book. Read it out loud so that group members can recall it:

"We all know what it feels like to excluded. We have all felt judged, pushed off to the side, categorized, or labeled. At the same time, we have all at some time or another participated in making someone else feel this way too. But the good news is that Jesus came to rescue us from all of this—to tear down the walls and blur the lines that the world uses to separate and divide and to bring us into a unified kingdom of God."

Ask: How does this quote encourage you? How does this quote challenge you?

ON THE OUTSIDE LOOKING IN

(10 minutes)

Instruct group members to turn to pages 119–121 in the journal, where they will find questions to help them reflect further on the inside-out nature of God's kingdom in the present world. Allow two minutes each (6 minutes total) for group members to respond to the questions in the space provided, with either drawn or written answers. Using a watch or clock to keep the time, tell group members when to move to the next question, even if they are not yet finished with the one they're working on. Here are the question (they are also printed in the journal):

1. When have you felt like you've been left out? Why does it feel so painful to be on the outside looking in? (2 minutes)

2. How does the way of the world differ from the kingdom of God? (2 minutes)

3. What possibilities do you see for reaching out to those who are on the outside of your group or outside of the church? (2 minutes)

After the six minutes, invite group members to share their responses.

MULTIPLICATION AND MISSION

(15 minutes)

Ask for a volunteer to summarize the teaching on the purpose of the church from Matthew 16 on pages 107–109 of the journal.

Read the following quote from page 108 in the journal out loud:

"Jesus envisioned his church reaching out to a lost and broken world, not retreating from it. We tend to identify ourselves as Christian based on the amount of distance we can keep between the world and ourselves, but where is Jesus going to build his church? Right in the middle of the world and all its mess."

Ask: In what ways are you and our church "right in the middle of the world and all its mess"? What can we do in our group and as individuals to embody this teaching more fully?

Ask group members to turn to pages 122–123 in the journal. Explain that you will spend a few minutes reading over the two passages, Acts 2:42-47 and Acts 4:32-37. Yes, you have spent a lot of time with these passages over the last few weeks. But they have so much to teach us about our how we can make the most out of our life together!

Invite group members to make notes on these passages in the space provided, using the following questions as prompts (these are also printed in the journal):

1. Where do you see evidence of multiplication in these passages?

2. Where do you see evidence of mission in these passages?

3. How can your small group community demonstrate the inside-out nature of the gospel that we see described in these passages?

Allow seven or eight minutes for members to read and respond individually in the space provided in the journal. Then invite group members to share their responses and insights on these three questions.

In your discussion, you may wish to reference the teaching about multiplication and mission on pages 105–109 of the journal.

Note: The conversation about multiplication is one that tends to make people uneasy. That is usually because what they have in their mind is the group splitting right down the middle and then never seeing each other again. That isn't how it has to go. Instead, the vision is usually for groups to send out one or two people from their midst to go and start a new group for folks who are on the outside looking in. At the same time, there can be some sort of relationship between the old and new groups. Most importantly, friendships can stay intact even though you aren't in the same small group community anymore. It is good to give this reassurance at the outset, even though as the journal says it's important not to rush too quickly into multiplication.

ONE CHALLENGE

(5 minutes)

The ONE Challenge this week is once again all about action. You as a group will put into practice what you have learned. Instruct each group member to identify someone who is "on the outside looking in"—who hasn't said yes to the saving love of God. The goal for this week will be to identify someone, a person or perhaps a group of people, and also think through how to share the good news of Jesus Christ with them.

Tell the group to bring these ideas to the next meeting, so that you can discuss what it might mean for you to share the good news of God's kingdom with those who haven't heard it or haven't responded to it.

CLOSE THE MEETING

(2 minutes)

Remind the group about your next session, as well as the daily devotionals for the upcoming week.

Ask a volunteer to close the meeting with a prayer.

Part 2:

WEEKS 5–8

A Word to the Leader

Congratulations on making this far! At this point, there is a pretty big shift that needs to take place. Instead of leaning on the teaching in the journal and the video, your conversation will now be driven by the conversation among your group. Here is where asking good questions will be especially important for you as the leader. Good, timely questions can help guide the conversation, push people toward answers that are well-thought-out, and make the most out of your time together. Try not to let the people in the group get away with one-word answers. One way to do that is to follow up what seems like a simple answer with the request, "Tell us more about that." Another great way to deepen the conversation is to ask people to share personal examples of what they are talking about. The follow-up question, "Can you give us an example?" can work in a variety of situations to help your conversation go deeper.

Have courage! More than likely your time together so far will have created fertile soil for great connection to happen. Continue to pray for your group members and the remainder of your time together, and count it a blessing to be a part of this process as the group leader. You and your group are very likely well prepared to undertake this next stage in the curriculum, the next step toward becoming the kind of community that can really make a difference in one another's lives.

Session 5:

PUSHING ONE ANOTHER FORWARD

PREPARATION

For the next four weeks, it will be important for you to have some way to take and display notes on the group discussions that you all have, as well as a way to display your group's covenant statement as it begins to take shape. A large piece of paper and pen, a markerboard with markers, or even an electronic display will work well for this purpose. You will see in the session plan below where and how to use these materials. Be sure to have them available in your meeting space before the session begins, in addition to the pens, pencils, extra journals, and Bibles.

As always, review the session beforehand to familiarize yourself with it. Be sure to arrive to your meeting space early, and start on time.

THE THREE QUESTIONS

(15 minutes)

In helping to enrich this conversation, feel free to refer back to the daily devotionals on each of these questions.

You'll also notice that a little more time is devoted to the Three Questions this week than in weeks past. As you get more comfortable with the questions, you may decide to spend more time on them. You may even decide to answer all three for each person rather than choosing just one. Extra time has been built in for that reason. You should not feel rushed, though you should take care that each person has approximately the same amount of time to respond as everyone else. Remember, these Three Questions are not preliminary icebreakers before the "real work" begins. They are a vital part of the real work, and the connections that happen through them are significant, as I hope you've come to see over the past several weeks.

Use a method of your own choosing to determine who will answer the question(s) in which order, and which question(s) you will answer. Refer back to this section in previous weeks for ideas for how you might proceed with your group.

Ask one, two, or all of the Three Questions and allow everyone in the group to respond:

1. What are you grateful for?

2. What are you anxious about?

3. What are you learning?

ONE CHALLENGE FOLLOW-UP

(5 minutes)

Check in with the group briefly on the ONE Challenge from this past week. Who did each person identify as someone who might be "on the outside looking in?" What might you as a group, or group members individually, do to share God's love with them?

MISSION STATEMENTS

(8 minutes)

Ask the group to turn to page 134 in the journal to consider the mission statements that are printed there. Read each mission statement out loud, and invite participants to circle which company uses that for a mission statement. The correct answers are **bold** in this leader guide, but not in the journals.

1. "To be one of the world's leading producers and providers of entertainment and information. We seek to develop the most creative, innovative and profitable entertainment experiences and related products in the world."

a. Gerber
b. Walt Disney
c. Pixar

2. "To be Earth's most customer-centric company where people can find and discover anything they want to buy online."

a. Zappos
b. Amazon
c. Frito-Lay

3. "To give people the power to share and make the world more open and connected."

a. Facebook
b. AT&T
c. ADT Home Security

4. "To bring inspiration and innovation to every athlete in the world."

a. Dunkin' Donuts
b. Icy Hot
c. Nike

Ask: How easy or difficult was it to identify the correct company for each mission statement? Why was this?

Ask a group member to read or summarize the teaching about mission statements on page 135 in the journal.

Ask: In light of this, what should be our goals for writing a covenant statement, which will serve as the mission statement for our group? How will the covenant statement reflect our identity and purpose?

Tell the group that over the next three weeks, you will discuss each of the three Core Practices deeply and identify the shape that these practices will take in your small group. This work will inform you all as you develop your covenant statement, which will take shape over the next several weeks. By the end of week 7, you will likely have a group covenant statement completed. Even if you don't have it all the way finished, you will be well on your way and be prepared to finish it with relative ease.

PUSHING ONE ANOTHER FORWARD

(20 minutes)

The focus for this session is on the first Core Practice, pushing one another forward. For the next ten minutes or so of this session, you will spend time reflecting on this core practice through prompts in the journal. These individual reflections will form the basis of your discussion as you develop the first part of your covenant statement.

Ask participants to turn to pages 136–138 in the journal and locate the prompts at the top of each page. Tell the group to write or draw their responses to these questions, letting them know that they'll have the next twenty minutes to do this. Though this may sound like a lot of time, it will allow for some deep thought and careful reflection.

Here is where the previous week's devotional can really come in handy. It was written in order to prepare the group to talk about this practice. Be sure to refer the group back to it before you set them to work on their own to answer the following prompts.

Keep track of the time using a watch or a clock, and give updates after three, five, and eight minutes have passed.

After the ten minutes are up, gather everyone back together to discuss your responses and work toward a covenant statement in the section below.

Note: This session is written as if all participants will remain in the same room and work individually, side-by-side. As an alternative, if space allows you may wish to send people out of the room to go off by themselves to answer these prompts. Be aware that if you do this, people will have to keep track of the time by themselves, and it may take a little bit longer to gather everyone back together for a discussion.

Discuss your responses to the journal prompts as a group. Ask the questions below, inviting group members to share their journal reflections and drawings as they answer.

Ask: What words, phrases, or pictures came to mind when you thought about the practice of pushing one another forward?

Ask: How you have experienced being pushed forward in a negative way? How have you seen this practice do damage or cause hurt, whether to you or someone else?

Ask: How have you have experienced being pushed forward in a positive way? How have you seen this practice help heal and transform someone?

During this discussion, be sure to pay attention to any similar words, phrases, ideas, or experiences that multiple group members have. Pay close attention also to different, perhaps conflicting perspectives on this first Core Practice. Now is the time to get everyone's expectations out on the table in order to avoid misunderstandings down the road.

CASE STUDY:
PUSHING ONE ANOTHER FORWARD

(10 minutes)

After you have discussed the group's responses in the journal about pushing one another forward, review the following case study to prepare you for developing this part of your covenant statement. This will help keep your creative juices flowing. More importantly, it will help you to think through how this Core Practice can and should be applied in real life situations.

Explain that you will read a statement from a hypothetical person, who explains a little bit about his faith situation. Encourage the group to listen actively to the statement and think through how they will push this person forward.

Read the following statement out loud to the group, or ask a volunteer to read it:

"I've been going to church most of my life. Being in a small group is new to me, but I've always known I needed to have others involved in my life. So, I'm glad I have this group. It has been probably a year since I actually read the Bible for myself. In fact it has been months since I've actually spent time praying. To be honest, I don't miss it. I think some of you remember that my girlfriend broke up with me about six months ago. Ever since then I have been pretty angry with God. I don't know if I am trying to get even with God or something, but I just feel like doing any of those spiritual things is a big waste of time. Maybe all this does have to do more with me than with God though. I don't know. I guess I just need your help."

Ask: What kinds of needs are present in this circumstance? Physical? spiritual? emotional? relational?

Ask: What might it look like to push this person forward?

Ask: What kinds of obstacles do you anticipate to pushing this person forward?

Ask: If you were in this situation described above, how would you want the group to respond?

Ask: How do your own reflections in the journal that we just discussed tell you about what type of response might be needed?

Ask: How might your covenant statement help guide the group in this situation?

Use this last question as a transition to working on your group's covenant statement using the guidelines below.

HOW ARE YOU GOING TO DO IT?

(20 minutes)

For the remainder of this session, you and the group will do the hard work of crafting the first part of your covenant statement. What shape will the Core Practice of pushing one another forward take for your group?

Ask: Based on our discussion, what will we do to push one another forward?

Page 139 of the journal will have a few ideas, but these are intended only to spark your imagination. Lead the group in brainstorming to arrive at your own way to carry out this practice.

As the discussion progresses, use a markerboard, large piece of paper, or electronic display to take notes and hone in on the final wording of this part of your covenant statement.

The goal for this time is for you to arrive at an established practice for pushing one another forward, which will become a part of your group's covenant statement. There is space in the journal (page 139) for you all to write this down. It is also a good idea for you to post this part of the covenant statement, again on a large piece of paper, markerboard, or electronic display. Keep this up each week, adding to it as your covenant statement grows. It will serve as a reminder of last week's discussion and consensus, and it will help you track your progress.

NOTE: Your group may not have enough time to finalize this part of your covenant statement before the end of today's session. If that is the case, don't worry. You can revisit it at a later date as one of your first priorities as you continue meeting after the end of the ONE Curriculum.

CLOSE THE SESSION

(2 minutes)

Before you leave, be sure to emphasize the importance of the group coming ready and willing to engage in the conversation. Utilizing the devotionals and revisiting the material from the previous sessions will help everyone to do that.

Ask a volunteer to close the session with a word of prayer.

Session 6:

LIFTING ONE ANOTHER UP

This week you will continue working on your group's covenant statement by focusing on the second Core Practice, lifting one another up. Like last week, your group's conversation will drive most of the lesson. Remember the importance of asking good questions and of everyone in the group committing to this process!

PREPARATION

Be sure that you have the first part of your group's covenant statement to display in your meeting space. This will help remind everyone what you discussed last week, and you can add to it through today's discussion. Gather the materials (markerboard, large paper, or electronic display) for taking notes during your discussion as well.

Bring your other supplies, such as pens or pencils, extra copies of the journal, Bibles, and anything else you might need. Be sure to start the session on time.

THE THREE QUESTIONS

(15 minutes)

Begin by checking in with anything from last week's Three Questions that may need some follow-up. Did someone share something that requires accountability from the group? Or maybe there is someone with a real tangible need that was shared. Has that need been met? It's not only important to share needs among the group but also to meet these needs for one another as well as you are able.

After following up from last week, ask and answer the Three Questions in your group this week.

1. What are you grateful for?

2. What are you anxious about?

3. What are you learning?

You as the leader decide how you will proceed in answering the questions, whether group members will answer one, two, or all three. Just make sure that everyone has a chance to answer and that the group gives equal attention to everyone's responses.

DO YOU TRUST ME?

(10 minutes)

Ask the group, "Who has a dollar?" When someone presents the dollar, take the money from them and ask, "Do you trust me?" If they say yes, give the dollar to another person in the group.

Repeat the exercise, but this time ask for a five dollar bill. After someone gives it to you, ask that person, "Do you trust me?" Again if they say yes, give the five dollar bill to another person in the group.

Repeat the exercise a final time, this time asking for a twenty dollar bill. After someone gives it to you, ask, "Do you trust me?" If they say yes, give the twenty dollar bill to someone else in the group.

Conclude this exercise by returning each sum of money to its original owner. Then discuss the following questions:

Ask: What risks were our friends taking when they presented their money to me?

Ask: Those of you who gave the money, what kind of feelings did you have when it was taken and given to someone else?

Ask: What kind of feelings did you have when it was returned?

Ask: What kind of relationship do the words *risk* and *trust* have with one another?

Ask: What part does risk play in vulnerability, compassion, and grace?

Say: Trust is such a vital aspect of the practice of lifting one another up. Each participant must believe that the others have his or her best interest in mind. Each participant must also prove to be trustworthy in staying confidential in the group's dealings and in being available when there is a need. Keep this in mind as we think through how lifting one another up might take shape in our group.

LIFTING ONE ANOTHER UP

(20 minutes)

The focus for this session is on the second Core Practice, lifting one another up. For the next ten minutes of this session, group members will use the journal to reflect individually on this core practice. Then you will all use these insights to fuel your discussion as you develop the second part of your covenant statement.

Ask participants to turn to pages 151–153 in the journal and locate the prompts at the top of each page. Instruct the group to write or draw their answers to these questions in the space provided, and remind them that they'll have ten minutes to do this. Encourage participants to recall and rely upon on the daily devotionals from this past week. What from their reading challenged or encouraged them in their understanding of this practice?

Keep track of the time using a watch or a clock, and give updates after three, five, and eight minutes have passed.

After the ten minutes are up, gather everyone back together to discuss your responses and work toward a covenant statement in the section below.

Note: Like last week, you may choose to have participants leave the room and go off by themselves to complete these exercises.

Invite everyone back together and discuss your responses to the journal prompts as a group.

Ask: What words, phrases, or pictures come to mind when you think about the practice of lifting one another up?

Ask: How have you have experienced being lifted up, or lifting someone else up, in a negative way? How have you seen this practice do damage or cause hurt?

Ask: How have you experienced being lifted up, or lifting someone else up, in a positive way? How have you seen this practice help heal and transform people?

Note any similarities that emerge in your discussion, which could be a clue that this is an important aspect of lifting one another up for several members of your group. Pay attention also to potential sources of misunderstanding or conflict, so that you can address them as you craft this next part of your covenant statement.

CASE STUDY:
LIFTING ONE ANOTHER UP

(10 minutes)

After you have discussed the group's responses in the journal about the second Core Practice, review the following case study to prepare you for developing this part of your covenant statement. Like last week's case study, this exercise will help you to think through how you can lift one another up in real life situations.

Explain that you will read a statement from a hypothetical person, who explains a little bit about her life circumstances recently. Encourage the group to listen actively to the statement and think through how they will push this person forward.

Read the following statement out loud to the group, or ask a volunteer to read it:

"It's been a pretty wild couple of weeks. I know I haven't been here for a while, but we've just had a lot going on. A couple of days ago I was let go from my job. I don't want you all to overreact. We are going to be fine. We have some money in savings to hold us over and I'm already out there talking to people and sending out resumes. I'm just telling you all of this to keep us in your prayers. It's going to be tight for a while, especially if I can't find work, but we will just have to adjust. The hardest thing for me, to be honest, is feeling like I'm not pulling my weight. I've had a good job for over twenty years. I've been a provider. I feel like a bit of a failure. I'm probably just feeling sorry for myself. I just need to suck it up and keep looking. Once I have that job again I know it will all be good."

Ask: What kinds of needs do you see in the statement above? Physical? spiritual? emotional? relational?

Ask: What would it look like to lift up this person?

Ask: What kinds of obstacles do you see to lifting this person up?

Ask: If you were in this situation described above, how would you want the group to respond?

Ask: Based on your own reflections in the Journal that we just discussed, what insights do you have about what type of response might be needed?

Ask: How might your covenant statement help guide the group in this situation?

Use this last question as a transition to begin working on your group's covenant statement using the guidelines below.

HOW ARE YOU GOING TO DO IT?

(20 minutes)

For the rest of this session, your group will develop and write the second part of your covenant statement. How will you take up the Core Practice of lifting one another up?

Ask: Based on our discussion, how will we lift one another up?

Use a markerboard, large piece of paper, or electronic display to take notes and make any preliminary drafts of this part of your covenant statement.

The goal once again this week is for you to determine your group's specific practice of lifting one another up, and this will become a part of your group's covenant statement. As you finish it, there is space in the journal (page 154) for you to write this down. Be sure also to add it to your display from last week, so you can see how your covenant statement is taking shape.

NOTE: If your group is unable to finish this part of your covenant statement in the allotted time, that is OK. You can return to this discussion at a later time after the end of the ONE Curriculum, making it one of the first things you do as you continue to meet together. Resist the temptation to ask the group to stay late to work on this until it is finished. It is important that you allow the group meeting to end on time this week, and every week, to maintain a consistent meeting time.

CLOSE THE SESSION

(2 minutes)

Remind everyone once again of the importance of engaging deeply in the conversation and preparing throughout the week with the daily devotionals, revisiting some of the teaching content from the first four weeks if necessary. Your group will be stronger the more you all put into it!

Ask a volunteer to close the session with prayer.

Session 7:

SENDING ONE ANOTHER OUT

This week you will work to finalize your group's covenant statement by discussing in depth the third Core Practice, sending one another out. This is vital for your group if you are to follow the example of the early church and be the kind of community that receives the goodwill of everyone around you (see Acts 2:47).

Remember, the good news of Jesus Christ and the kingdom of God is always going beyond itself; its direction is outward. In this session, you will determine how your group will express that ever-outward movement of God's kingdom.

PREPARATION

Set up the first two parts of your group's covenant statement in your meeting space. In addition to reminding everyone what you have discussed over the last two weeks, this will help you see the full finished statement when you have crafted the third part of it at the end of today's session. Gather the materials (markerboard, large paper, or electronic display) for taking notes during your discussion as well.

Be sure that you start on time and bring the other supplies that you need, including pens or pencils, extra copies of the journal, and Bibles.

THE THREE QUESTIONS

(15 minutes)

As you did last week, check in with your group members if anything was raised last week during this time that someone needed to follow up on. Have needs been met and gratitude shared? Is there an ongoing concern that someone wants to give an update on? Engaging in this way with one another helps the Three Questions become a real tool for sharing your lives with one another and drawing the whole group together. It may be that such follow-up is not needed right now, but keep the practice in mind so that you will remember to use it when it is needed in the future.

After checking in from last week, ask and answer the Three Questions in your group once again.

1. What are you grateful for?

2. What are you anxious about?

3. What are you learning?

If you've been answering only one of the questions each week, now is a good time to make sure that you are using all of the questions. Does one person (or several people, or the whole group) tend to answer one question most of the time when he or she is given the choice? Or have you noticed that several people consistently shy away from one of the questions? If so, gently point this out and encourage people to answer a question that challenges them in a new way.

GOOD NEWS

(10 minutes)

Good news demands that it be shared, and the truth is that we are really good at sharing it. Sharing good news with others just comes naturally to us. Let's have a little fun with this by taking a moment to play a game of charades as a group.

Give six people within your group some sort of "good news" that they must share with everyone. Write each bit of good news on a piece of paper and hand them to your group members, taking care that each member's piece of good news remains a secret. Ask for a volunteer to begin.

Instruct the volunteer to share his or her bit of good news with the group. The only catch is, this person must share his or her news through body language only. No talking or noises! While the volunteer does his or her best silent acting job, encourage the group to try to guess the "good news" as quickly as possible. Don't be shy let—let your inner thespians shine!

Pieces of good news:

a.   I got the job!

b.   We won the game!

c.   I'm engaged!

d.   I'm pregnant!

e.   I graduated!

f.   I love you!

After the game of charades is finished, discuss the following questions:

Ask: What makes good news so exciting to share with others?

Ask: When was a time in your life that you had good news you could not wait to share?

Say: "Sending one another out is all about sharing the good news of Jesus Christ with others. Once again, we will apply the same exercises we have been using in the previous sessions to talk about the practice of sending one another out. Our journal reflections and discussions will help us to develop this final part of our covenant statement."

SENDING ONE ANOTHER OUT

(20 minutes)

The focus for this session is on the third Core Practice, sending one another out. As with the last two weeks, group members will use the journal to reflect individually on this core practice, allowing about ten minutes for this process. Then you will discuss your responses as a group and work to develop the final part of the group's covenant statement.

Ask participants to turn to pages 165–167 in the journal and locate the prompts at the top of each page. Instruct the group to write or draw their answers to these questions in the space provided, and tell them that they'll have ten minutes to do so. Remind the group of the daily devotionals from this past week, encouraging them to use these to guide and inform their reflections.

Keep track of the time using a watch or a clock, and give updates after three, five, and eight minutes have passed.

After the ten minutes are up, gather everyone back together to discuss your responses and work toward a covenant statement in the section below.

Note: As before, you may choose to have participants leave the room and go off by themselves to complete these exercises if space allows.

Invite everyone back together and discuss your responses to the journal prompts as a group.

Ask: What words, phrases, or pictures come to mind when you think about the practice of sending one another out?

Ask: How have you experienced the practice of sending one another out in a negative way? Has someone sent you out, or have you sent someone else out, in a way that caused harm?

Ask: How have you experienced the practice of sending one another out in a positive way? Has someone sent you out, or have you sent someone else out, in a way that led to transformation and positive change?

CASE STUDY:
SENDING ONE ANOTHER OUT

(10 minutes)

After you have discussed the group's responses in the journal about sending one another out, review the following case study to prepare you for developing this last part of your covenant statement. As we have done the past two weeks, we will use this study as an exercise to help you think about this Core Practice from the perspective of a real life situation.

Explain that you will read a statement from a hypothetical person, who explains a little bit about his life recently. Encourage the group to listen actively to the statement and think through how they will send this person out.

Read the following statement out loud to the group, or ask a volunteer to read it:

> "Well my wife and I are very excited to be a part of this group. For years we have helped with high school kids at the church, but when our son went to college last year we kind of dropped off the scene. I retired last year too, so it has been an adjustment to figure out how to use all of my extra time. Sometimes I find myself mowing the lawn three times a week because I cannot stand to watch one more daytime drama. Anyway, it is good to see some of you we have not seen in a while because we have had trouble making it to church on the weekend. We don't really have an excuse, we just have slept in here and there and have traveled a bit. We knew we were missed in the pews when the pastor called to ask us to consider helping with a service project. We turned him down. Just could not fit it in the schedule. But we have been talking lately and feel like there are better ways to use this new freedom of schedule. We just are not sure how. But don't worry, we have stayed involved. We still tithe every week."

Ask: What kinds of needs are present in this circumstance? Physical? spiritual? emotional? relational?

Ask: What might it look like to send this person out?

Ask: What kinds of obstacles do you see to sending out this person?

Ask: If you were in this situation described above, how would you want the group to respond?

Ask: What do your own reflections in the journal that we just discussed tell you about what type of response might be needed?

Ask: How might your covenant statement help guide the group in this situation?

Use this last question as a transition to begin working on your group's covenant statement using the guidelines below.

HOW ARE YOU GOING TO DO IT?

(20 minutes)

After you have wrapped up the discussion, turn your attention to the formation of the covenant statement below. How will you take up the Core Practice of sending one another out? Use the large paper, markerboard, or electronic display to take notes, and work through the draft of this part of your covenant statement.

Ask: Based on our discussion, how will we send one another out?

Please be aware, this last part of your covenant statement may take some time to develop. You don't want the group to jump at any sort of cause that comes along, but to form a sense of what sort of issue you are best positioned to address. What are you as a group passionate about, and what will you be able to accomplish effectively with regards to this passion? I have found that three questions in particularly are especially effective to lead groups to identify a common cause that they can invest in. Consider asking these questions as a part of your discussion to guide the group:

What makes you angry?

What are the things in your community or the world that cause you to say, "That shouldn't happen!"? Often God's call comes to us from places of disruption, when we become suddenly aware of the fact that something is wrong and something must be done about it.

What do you love to do?

What are you passionate about? What is that thing you can get lost in? Or what do you as a group have to offer? What special skills or resources are at your disposal? Get creative on how you can combine the two of these things in order to make a difference for the Kingdom.

Where do we start?

What does a first step look like? Is there a person at your church or an organization you can reach out to in order to get some direction on how to invest in this particular cause?

Again, this may take some time to develop, and you may not be able to accomplish it all in this session. But make sure that you are carving out some time to talk about this as you continue to meet. As the leader, pay attention to what the members of your group are sharing. More than likely you will start to hear them talking about things going on in the world around them that bother them, or things that they wish were different. What we have to remember is that we may very well be the vessels through which God is going to bring change to these circumstances.

If you are able to determine your group's practice of sending one another out by the end of this session, write it down on page 168 of the journal along with the rest of your covenant statement. Add it also to your display from previous weeks, which will give you a completed covenant statement if you've been able to work through everything thus far.

CLOSE THE SESSION

(5 minutes)

Spending some time in prayer together, asking God to solidify the commitments that are being made by everyone in the group. If you have completed your covenant statement, recite it together as a group.

Ask God to help you maintain your commitment to this covenant and to one another.

It will be good for you to renew your commitment to this covenant periodically, at least once a year, to remind everyone what you all have signed up for.

After you have read and committed yourselves to your covenant statement, remind everyone that next week will be your last session. Encourage the group to use the daily devotional and come prepared for some great conversation next time.

Ask a volunteer to close the session with prayer.

Session 8:

GROUND RULES AND LIFE STORIES

I n this final session of the ONE Curriculum, your group will work to develop some ground rules that will guide your interactions with one another. Together with your covenant statement, these ground rules will help everyone to have the same life, mind, heart, and direction as a Christ-centered community.

Keep in mind that although this is your last session of ONE, this will not be your last meeting as a group. This eighth week is not the end; it is the beginning! From here you will continue to meet, sharing your lives together through the Three Questions and sharing your stories with one another over the course of the next few weeks. You will be on your own as a group, but hopefully you will find that these relationships are worthwhile and that you are growing as a result of them.

As you being this last session, offer these words of encouragement and joy to your group members.

PREPARATION

Display your group's covenant statement in your meeting space, or as much of it as you have been able to complete. As you work toward forming ground rules for your time together going forward, it will be good to keep your covenant statement in mind as well. Gather the materials (markerboard, large paper, or electronic display) for taking notes during your discussion and for writing down your ground rules as you develop them.

Be sure that you start on time and bring the other supplies that you need, including pens or pencils, extra copies of the journal, and Bibles.

THE THREE QUESTIONS

(15 minutes)

Once again, begin the session by following up with any needs, concerns, or celebrations that were lifted up last week with the Three Questions. Then have everyone in the group ask and answer the Three Questions, either choosing one or answering all three. Be sure that the group actively listens and engages with one another's responses, allowing yourself plenty of time for this part of the session.

1. What are you grateful for?

2. What are you anxious about?

3. What are you learning?

DRAWING PICTURES

(10 minutes)

Ask the group to turn to page 180 of the journal and look at the incomplete drawing that is there. Without giving them any extra details, simply instruct them to complete the drawing.

Give everyone in the group three minutes to draw, and then have them share with the group what they drew and why.

Have the group vote on who completed the drawing in the best way, with the only guideline being that nobody can vote for his or her own drawing. Offer a small prize for the winner, such as a gift card or some good food, to the person who wins.

After you complete this exercise, discuss using the following questions:

Ask: What made this exercise hard to do?

Ask: Why didn't everyone's drawing turn out the same? Why were the finished drawings so different?

Ask: What insights does this exercise give you about the way we should spend our time together?

Explain that we all have different perspectives and approach a given task or situation differently, bringing a unique background, skill set, and knowledge base that others don't always share. Without some common ground to start from, these unique gifts can send us in all sorts of different directions. The ground rules for our group, together with the covenant statement, help to identify common ground. Personal rules will always differ, but if you can establish and adhere to some common ground rules, it will minimize conflict and everyone in the group will benefit from it.

THE GROUND RULES

(25 minutes)

Instruct the group to turn to pages 182–184 in the journal, taking note of the prompts at the top of each page. Give the group ten minutes to write or draw their answers to these prompts, reminding them to draw on their daily devotionals for guidance and inspiration. The group may stay together in one room, or if space allows you may send everyone off by themselves to work on these alone.

Keep track of the time, and give updates after three, five, and eight minutes have passed. At the end of the ten minutes, gather everyone back together to discuss you responses.

Ask: What are some of your own personal rules that you live by? What rules do you expect others to live by, either consciously or unconsciously?

Ask: What are some conflicts that can arise in a group when two or more people have different unspoken rules?

Ask: What are some possible ground rules that we can agree upon to help minimize group conflict?

HOW ARE YOU GOING TO DO IT?

(20 minutes)

After you have discussed your responses for a bit, brainstorm some ground rules that you can all agree upon. The third question above should give you some good ideas to start with. Write these down on a large piece of paper, markerboard, or electronic display. Encourage the group to take their own notes on pages 185–186 of the journal as well.

I'm sure that your group will have some ground rules that are unique to you, but there are some very common barriers that tend to crop up in the majority of groups. Here are a few suggested ones to discuss:

Attendance: It can be hard to establish trust with people who do not seem committed to the group, and a lack of attendance can signify a lack of commitment. What can help here is to talk about logistics as well—when and where you meet. Would meeting on an every other week basis be a good idea or a bad idea for your group? If you are a young couples group with a lot of young children, one suggestion would be for the men and women to meet separately on different days and times of the week. The bottom line is, be creative with this and be open to changing your rhythm when you need to.

The "Dominator": This is a person who tends to talk much more than other people, often dominating conversations week-to-week. This is something small-group leaders have been struggling with from the very beginning. The more you talk about this now, the less awkward it will be when you have to address it.

Confidentiality: Nothing erodes trust like a breach in confidentiality. I'm sure this will get brought up at the very beginning, but an important conversation for you and group will be how you will handle a breach in confidentiality.

Conflict Management: Being committed to pushing one another forward means that you are going to have some difficult conversations. How are you going to challenge one another? I know of some groups who have ground rules prohibiting accusatory statements. Instead, they speak from their perspective saying things like, "When you do this, it makes me feel like this." I know of other groups who are committed to being generous with each other. When a member of the group is offended by another member of the group, he or she must ask for more clarification, such as, "What did you mean by that comment?" and not assume that the other person is trying to be offensive.

Having these conversations before conflict arises is so valuable, and it can really help get your group started off on the right foot.

If you are able to establish some ground rules, write them all down and display them for everyone to see. Ask the group to write them down also on the final page of the journal, where space is provided for exactly this purpose.

Be aware that establishing your ground rules takes time, and you may very well need to tweak and adjust them as you seek to live out the three Core Postures together. You and the group will learn as you go, but commit right now to be the kind of group that works through conflict in order to grow closer together.

CLOSE THE SESSION AND LOOK FORWARD TO NEXT TIME!

(10 minutes)

Remind the group that you will meet again, either next week or according to a different schedule that you will decide on. The end of the ONE Curriculum is not an end, but a beginning of your ongoing life in Christian community with one another.

Review the section in the journal entitled "Where to Go From Here . . . " (pages 187–190) together. Below, you will find some additional guidance on sharing your stories and throwing a party. Review these practices, and decide together what you will do the next time you meet, whether it is finishing up your covenant statement and ground rules, or coming up with a plan to begin sharing your stories with one another. Be sure that you set a date, time, and place for your next meeting. If you'll be sharing your stories, decide on a tentative schedule for doing so. And keep it consistent, so that you all know what to plan on and can commit to this time on a regular basis.

Ask a volunteer to close the session with prayer.

SHARING YOUR STORIES

Some folks in your group may really be struggling with this. Assure them that they only have to share what they are comfortable with right now. Trust takes time. But it also takes risk, and so we must be willing to get at least a little uncomfortable at some point.

Strongly encourage the folks in your group to share their story in whatever format seems easiest for them. The suggestions in the journal may work well for everyone, or you may come up with a better way. The most important thing is for people get a sense of who is in their small-group community by hearing about their background.

It is important for you to set some clear guidelines for the story sharing time, such as how many stories will be shared each week, how long they should be, and how long the conversation about each story will last. For instance, you may decide that two stories will be shared each week, they must be ten to fifteen minutes long, and that you will then spend ten minutes discussing them afterward. This helps to keep things on track and everyone on the same page.

THROWING A PARTY

The people of God should throw the *best* parties.

When you hold a celebration, be sure to incorporate some sort of activity that gives the members of the group an opportunity to celebrate one another. A classic activity involves a ball of yarn. Whoever starts holds on to the string and says something they have appreciated about another person in the group. While still holding the string, that person will then toss the ball of yarn to the person they have just described. The second person then holds onto his or her piece of loose string, describes something he or she appreciates in another person, and throws the ball to that person. This repeats until everyone in the group has had a chance to share. The image of the yarn connecting everyone is a powerful one.

Your biggest job as a leader is to continue to hold out in front of the people how important your life together is. One of the key ways you can do this is by continually recognizing and celebrating what God is doing in your midst. When there is a breakthrough, or a need gets met, or a next step is taken, do not just let it pass by. Call it out. Name it. Celebrate it. What will keep your group committed to one another is seeing and feeling God's very presence in your midst.